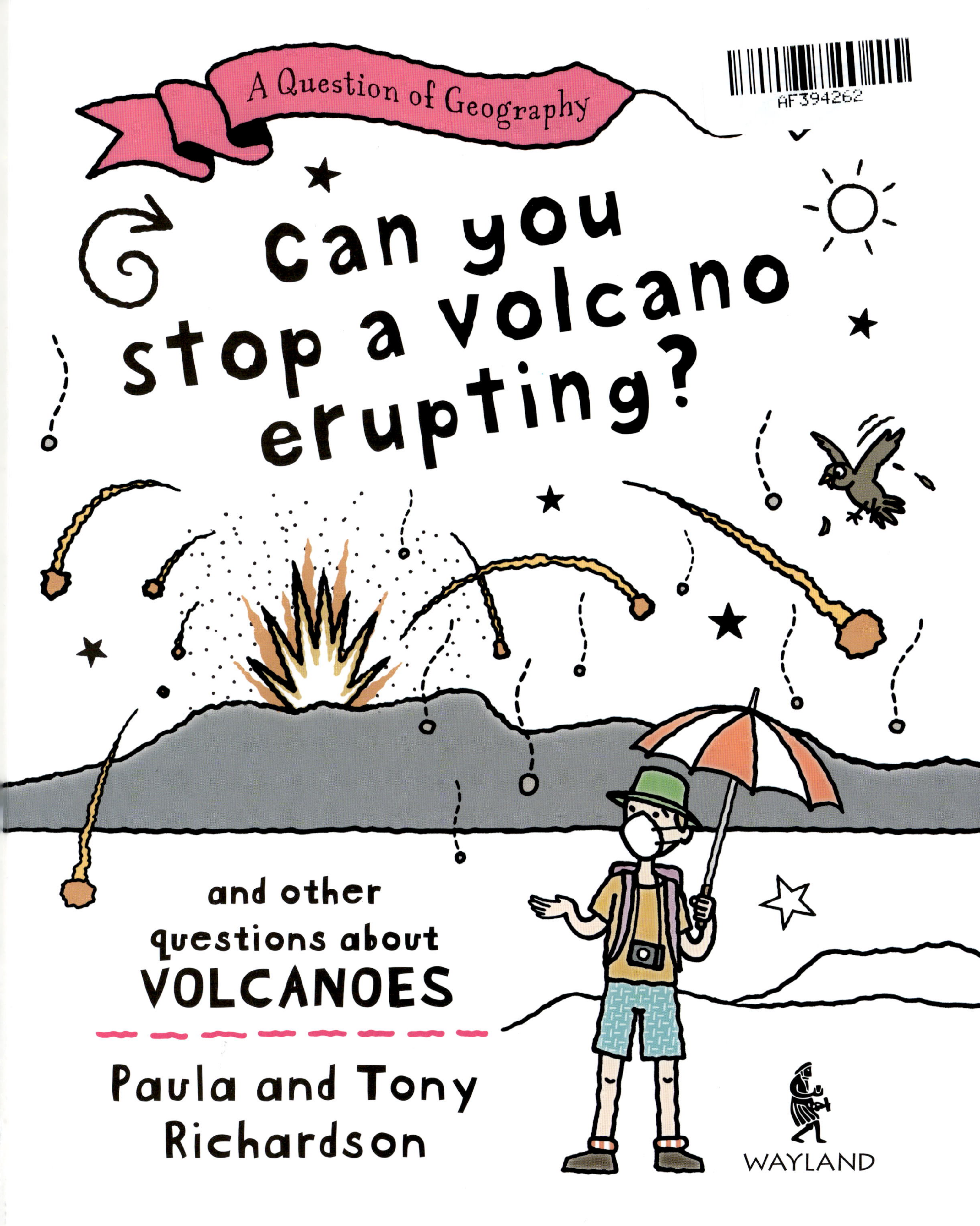

A Question of Geography
Can you stop a volcano erupting?
and other questions about VOLCANOES
Paula and Tony Richardson
WAYLAND
AF394262

First published in Great Britain in 2024
by Wayland

Credits:
Editors: Julia Bird; Julia Adams
Design and illustrations: Matt Lilly
Cover design: Matt Lilly

HB ISBN 978 1 5263 2593 8
PB ISBN 978 1 5263 2594 5

Printed and bound in Dubai

Picture credits:

Alamy: Arctic Images 27c; Bruno Compagnon/sagaphoto.com 27t;
Dennis Hallinan 10; Tom Pfeiffer 8; Tim Phillips 22l.
Getty Images: A Dagli Orti/DEA 19br; Oli Scarff 19bl.
NSF.gov: 23b.
Shutterstock: Zahirul Alwan 16t; David Herraez Calzada 25t;
Alexey Fedorenko 15; Sergii Figurnyi 20; Johann Helgason 13;
Marianna Ivanovska 22t; Roman Khomlyak 11; Kitnha 4;
leszczem 19c; Anna LoFi 12; Pallop Loharnchoon 23t;
Lyd Photography 25b; Alexander Magnum 16b; New Africa 21;
Norikko 28; Vincent Parkes 18; Sean Pavone 24t;Photoography 6;
OlgaPS 29; Georgio Rossi 23c; Toivido 14; Wead 19t;
Wirestock Creators 9.
USGS.gov: Michael Poland 22r.

Every effort has been made to clear copyright.
Should there be any inadvertent omission,
please apply to the publisher for rectification

Wayland
An imprint of
Hachette Children's Group
Part of Hodder and Stoughton Limited
Carmelite House
50 Victoria Embankment
London EC4Y 0DZ

An Hachette UK Company
www.hachette.co.uk
www.hachettechildrens.co.uk

The authorised representative in the EEA is
Hachette Ireland, 8 Castlecourt Centre,
Dublin 15, D15 XTP3, Ireland
(email: info@hbgi.ie)

Contents

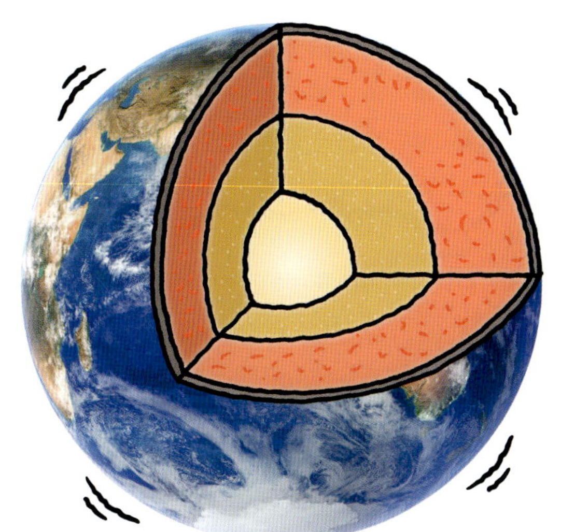

What are volcanoes?

Volcanoes are openings in Earth's crust where rock and gases from deep inside our planet can escape. Volcanoes helped to create the right conditions for life on our planet – without them there would be no you or me!

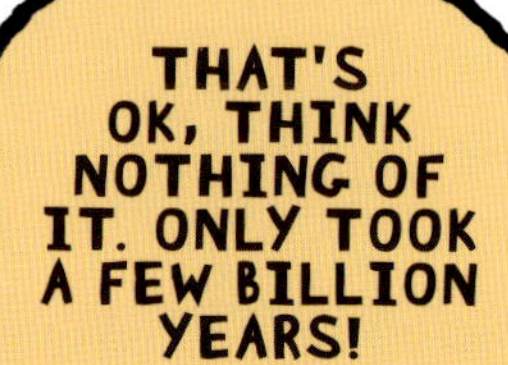

Today, there are around 550 active volcanoes on land and many more under the sea. As you read this, about 20 volcanoes are erupting somewhere in the world! This map shows where Earth's active volcanoes can be found.

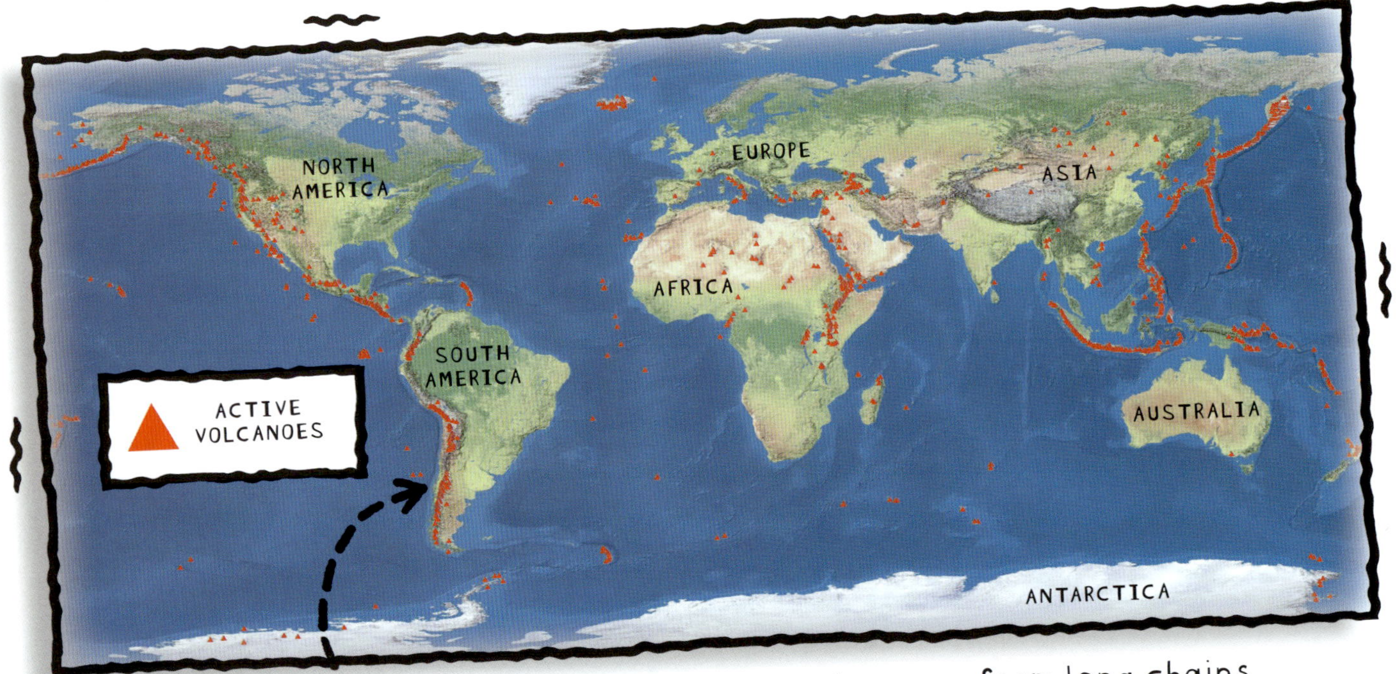

Notice that many of the volcanoes form long chains. This is a big clue as to how they formed!

Living on a crust

To explain how volcanoes are formed, we must look at the land we live on, called Earth's crust. This crust is about 35 to 40 kilometres thick on land, but as little as 6 km thick under the sea.

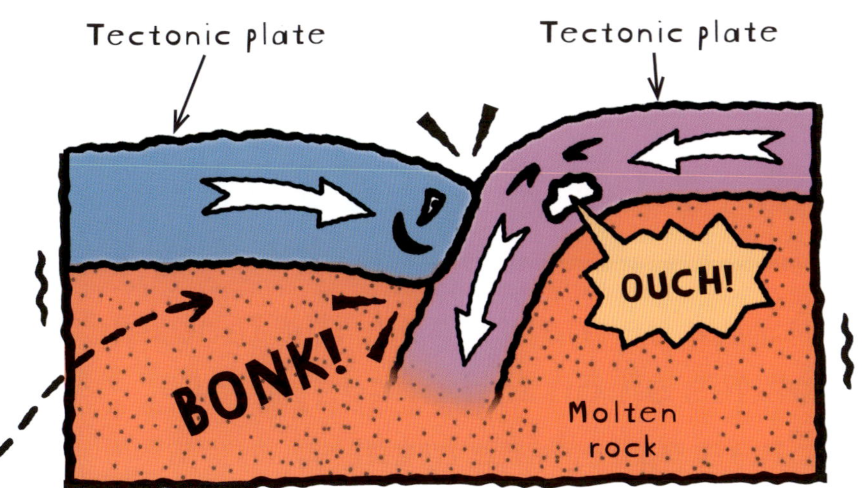

Piling on the pressure

Earth's crust is split up into gigantic pieces called tectonic plates. These float on the mantle, a layer of molten rock (magma). The movement of the magma moves the plates. Where they meet, **pressure** builds, making the plates grind against each other. Sometimes, they get stuck and then jolt apart, causing earthquakes. The pressure also creates cracks in the plates. It's through these cracks that magma pushes to the surface, forming a volcano.

The Ring of Fire

Many of the world's active volcanoes are located along the edges of the tectonic plates around the Pacific Ocean. They form a horseshoe-shaped area, known as the Ring of Fire. Countries within this area include those of North and South America, Japan, New Zealand and Pacific island states.

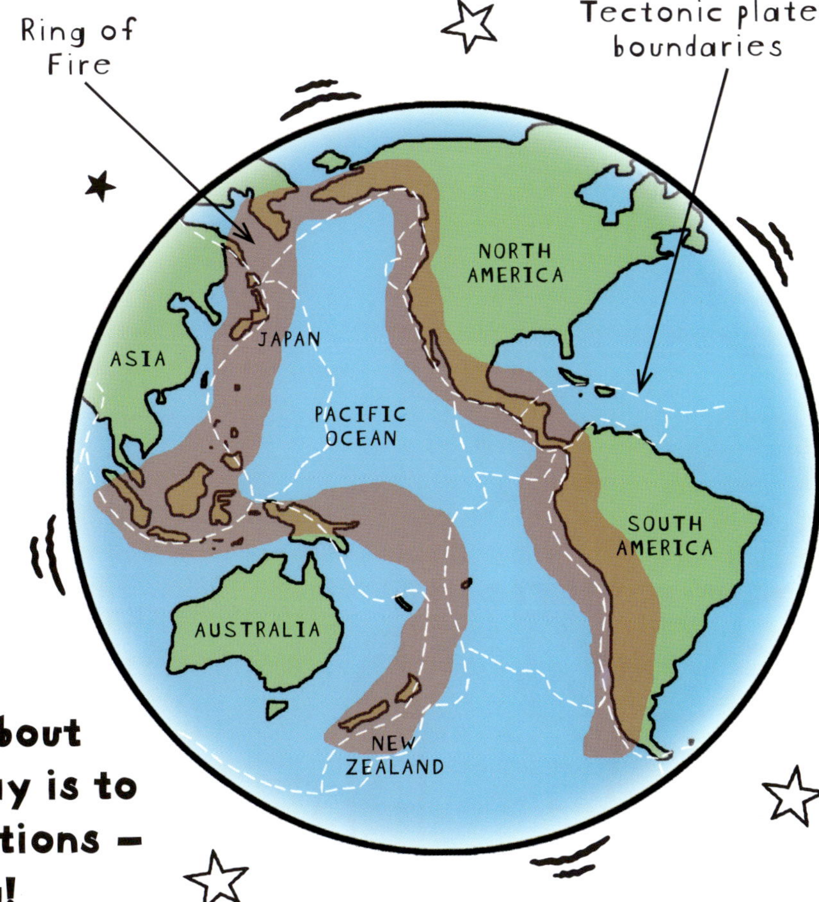

Want to learn more about volcanoes? The best way is to do that is by asking questions — so let's get asking!

Why is magma like a fizzy drink?

As we've mentioned, the tectonic plates sit on top of a layer of Earth called the mantle. The mantle contains magma – rock that is SO hot (about 1,980°C), it has become liquid.

WHOOSH!

Let me out!

When gases in the magma build up, the pressure builds and the magma becomes desperate to escape, a bit like the gases when you shake a bottle of fizzy drink!

Where two tectonic plates border each other, this high-pressured magma forces its way up from the mantle and then through cracks in the plates to erupt as a volcano. **BOOM!**

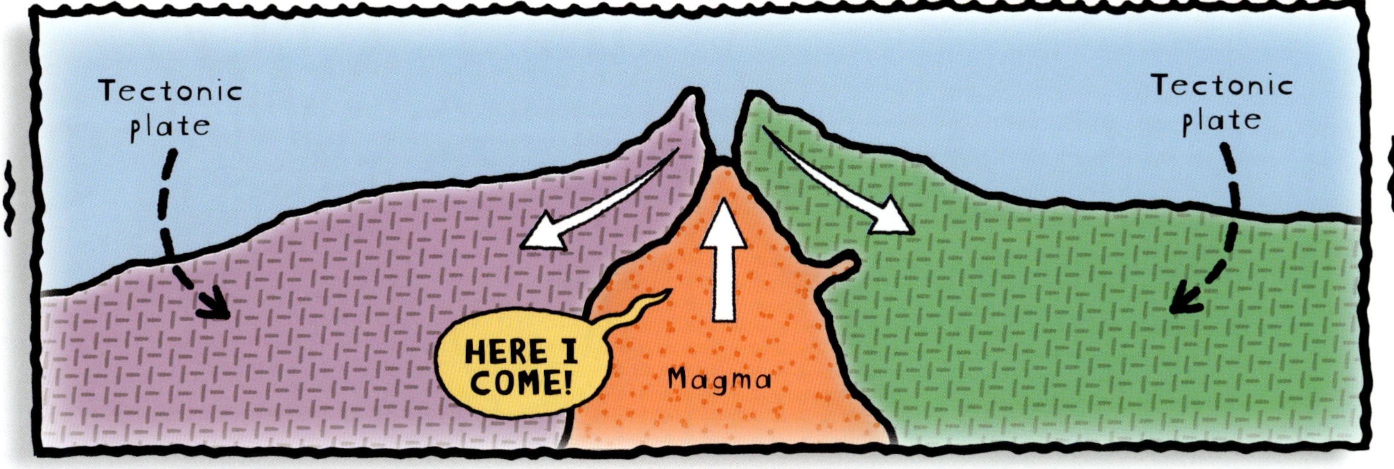

Thick or thin?

Magma comes in different consistencies, from thick and stodgy to thin and runny. Mixed with steam and other gases, it bursts out of Earth's surface through holes called vents. Often, one central vent creates a large hole at the top of a volcano, called a **crater**.

It is the difference in the magma's thickness and in the mix of water and gases that creates two types of volcanic eruption – **explosive** and **effusive**. These different eruptions form a variety of volcanoes (see pages 8–9).

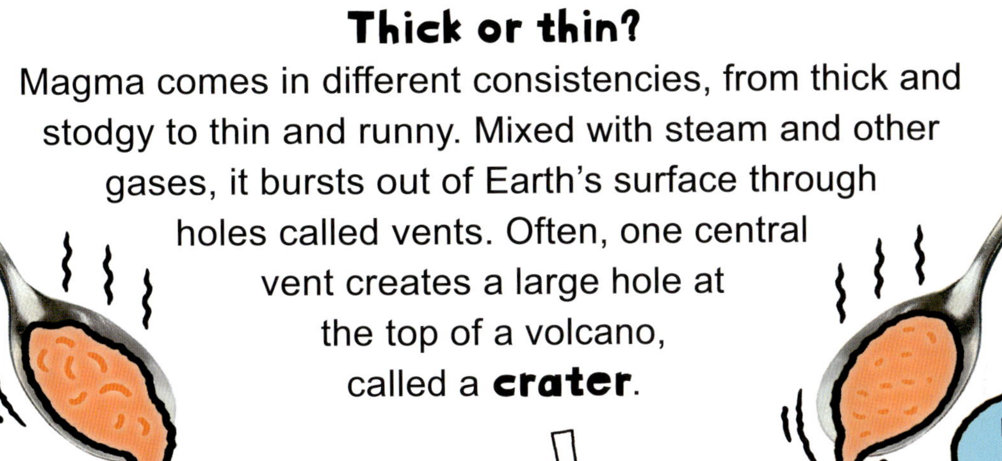

Once the magma emerges from the volcano it's called lava.

Composite, shield or cinder?

There are three main types of volcano and eruption.

Mount Etna erupting in 2014.

A **COMPOSITE VOLCANO** has explosive eruptions that are sudden and spectacular. Thick, stodgy magma traps water vapour and carbon dioxide gas, which heats up further and expands. The pressure becomes so great that it forces the magma to burst out. Once released, the volcano settles down for a while until the pressure builds up again.

Composite volcanoes are usually shaped like a cone, with layers of ash and lava building up after each eruption, creating steep sides. Mount Etna in Italy (left), and Mount Fuji in Japan are composite volcanoes.

Lava spilling out of the Hawaiian Mauna Loa shield volcano.

Effusive eruptions create a **SHIELD VOLCANO**. It gets its name because it looks like a rounded battle shield on its side. The magma is runny, like thin porridge. It creates lava that flows down the side of the volcano like a hot, molten river.

Where there is a LOT of dissolved gas and water in the magma, the lava is blasted out, shattering into fragments. These cool rapidly, forming a cloud of ash and cinder dust. This creates a cone around the crater, called a **CINDER VOLCANO**. This type of volcano can grow quite quickly, but is often smaller than other kinds of volcano.

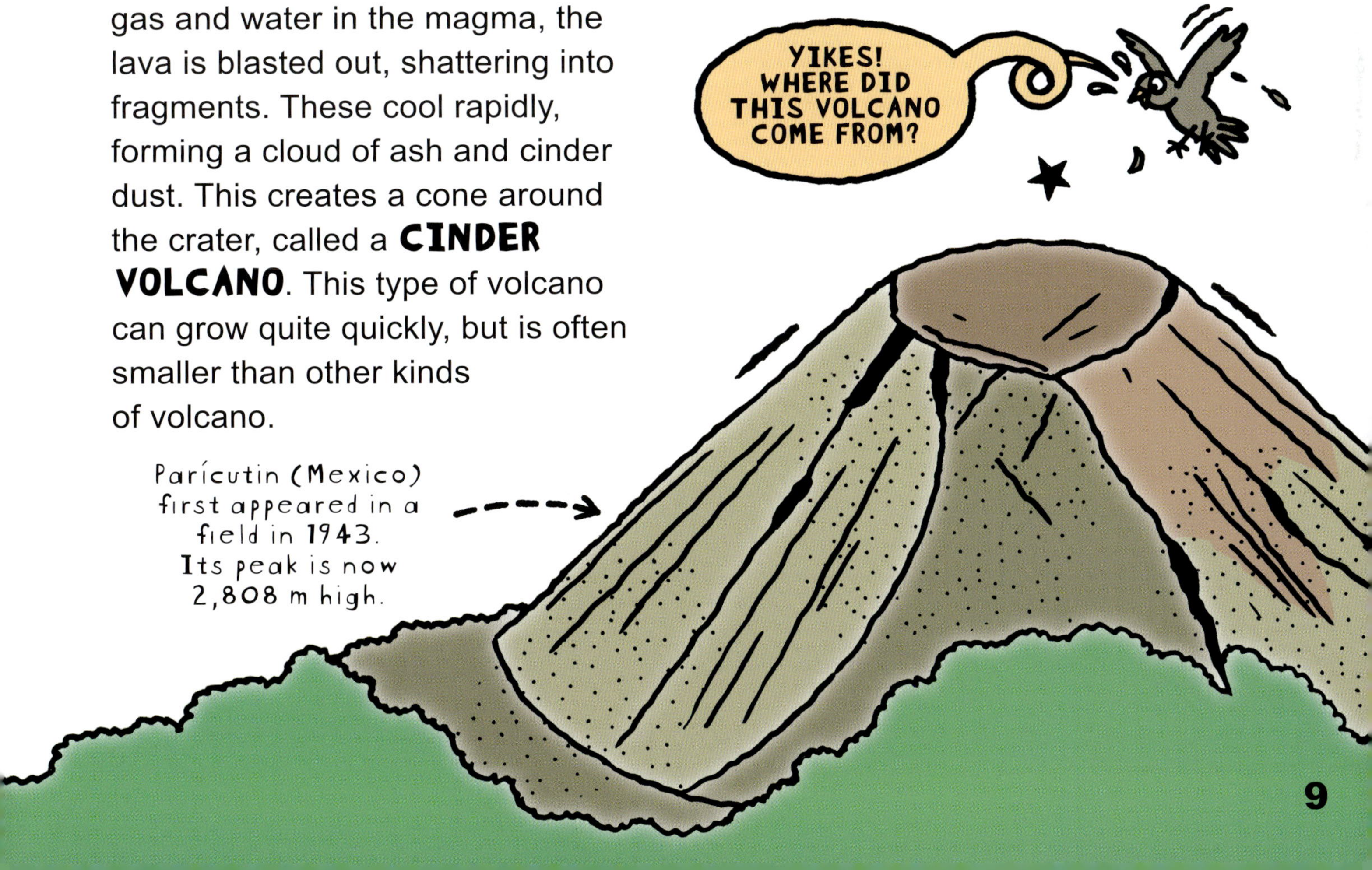

Parícutin (Mexico) first appeared in a field in 1943. Its peak is now 2,808 m high.

What woke up Mount St. Helens?

In May 1980, Mount St. Helens (also known as Lawetlat'la or Loowit) in North America suddenly erupted! For 123 years it had been quiet, so its explosive eruption was quite a shock.

Mount St. Helens before the eruption.

The build-up

While the volcano was dormant, it was a great tourist attraction for hikers and climbers. In the weeks leading up to the eruption, however, small tremors and earthquakes had started occurring.

Scientists realised that the earthquakes had released new magma from deep in the Earth. They warned people, and most evacuated. What no one expected was the ferocity of the eruption.

A volcano is **DORMANT** when it hasn't erupted for tens or hundreds of years, but potentially still could.

A mountain blown away!

On 18 May, nearly half of the mountain was blasted up into the sky, and with it, a huge cloud of very hot ash, dust, steam and gas. With a temperature of over 400°C, the cloud rolled down the mountain at tremendous speed, burning everything in its path. The ash was also blasted up to 20 km into the atmosphere.

Mount St. Helens today.

Whole areas of forest were destroyed by the ash cloud. Further down, torrents of mud, created by melted snow and ice mixing with the rock debris, clogged nearby river valleys. Because the eruption was far greater than expected, some people were caught out. Sadly, 57 people died, including scientists observing the volcano.

Under pressure

It was only discovered afterwards that the new magma inside Mount St. Helens had contained large amounts of steam. This created tremendous pressure inside the volcano. Enough to blow its top off!

How can a volcano spoil your holiday?

Very easily! Some volcanoes emit so much ash that the surrounding area is completely buried. The ash can also fly up into the atmosphere and travel for many miles.

Houses buried in volcanic ash in La Palma, Canary Islands.

Lights out!

Ash clouds can have a strange effect on the light coming from the Sun by creating an unusual red or orange glow. If the cloud is very thick, it can block out the Sun completely, making it seem as if it's night time. Not great for sun-bathing!

Volcano stops flights

In 2010, planes around the world had
to stop flying because an Icelandic
volcano erupted. It was spewing out so
much ash and dust that it threatened
to clog the engine of any plane that
flew near it. Thousands of flights were
cancelled, causing travel chaos.

The name of the volcano was:
(beware – difficult to pronounce
unless you're Icelandic!)

Eyjafjallajökull

You say it:
AY-yah-FYAH-dlah-YER-kutl !

Volcanoes take over the weather

History has shown that volcanic eruptions can affect the weather
for months or even years! Europe experienced
a year without summer in 1816 when
Mount Tambora, in Indonesia,
erupted and sent a dust
cloud over Europe.

This travelling dust
cloud blocked out the
light and heat of the
Sun, making the season
much colder. Important
food crops did not grow,
causing food shortages.

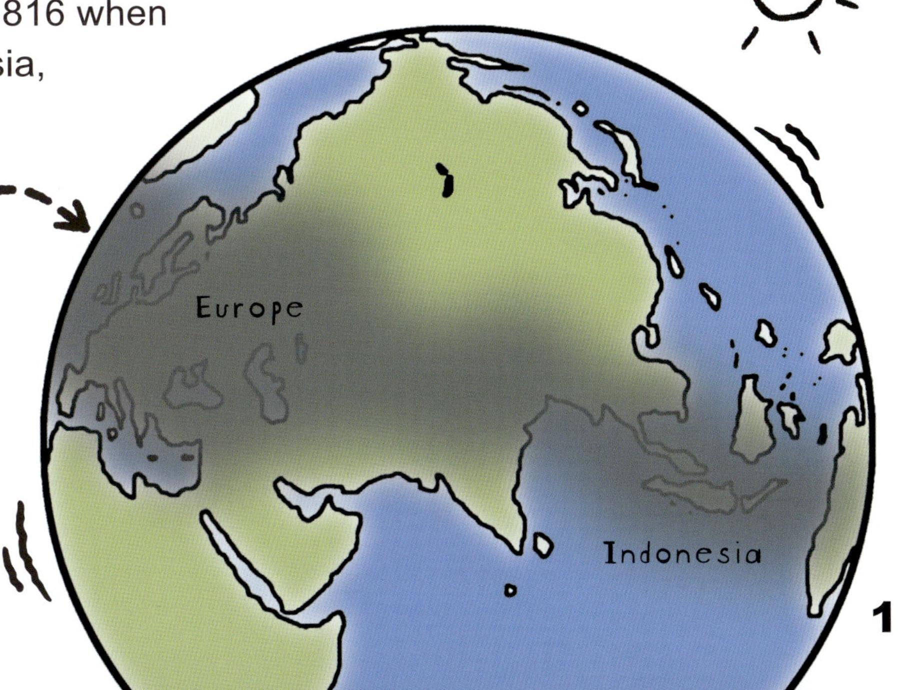

Can you stop a volcano erupting?

Sorry, but there is no way of stopping volcanoes from erupting. That hasn't stopped some brave people from trying, though!

Attempts have been made to stop lava flows destroying villages and towns by digging large trenches to change the direction of the flow, and even by dropping bombs on it.

Save the harbour!

The most successful attempt was made in Iceland in 1973. People living in the small town of Vestmannaeyjar on the island of Heimaey, were threatened by the erupting volcano Helgafell.

The harbour at Vestmannaeyjar today.

During the eruption, the residents pumped seawater to cool and divert the lava flow before it could clog the harbour, which is very important for the town's fishing industry. The idea worked! However, they still lost over 400 houses, which were buried by all the ash and rock that came raining down from the sky.

Time for a rest

A volcano will only stop erupting when the pressure underground eases. The volcano is then dormant, meaning it is at rest but could start erupting again in the future (see pages 10–11). If a volcano has not erupted for tens of thousands of years, it is known as extinct. However, even some extinct volcanoes have been known to wake up, especially if they are in earthquake areas along tectonic plate borders.

Put a plug in it!

At one time, there were volcanoes in the United Kingdom, but all are believed to be extinct now, the last having erupted 55 million years ago. All have lost contact with any source of magma.

That's good news for the city of Edinburgh in Scotland. The whole city lies in an ancient volcano and Edinburgh Castle was built on a rock called a plug, which sits in a volcano vent!

Is a volcano visit always a bad idea?

Well, some volcanoes can be visited quite safely. Vesuvius in Italy has thousands of visitors a year. But just in case, here are a few things to be aware of when you are visiting an active volcano!

Cough! Splutter!

Ash and dust can spew out for days, gradually building up like an extremely heavy fall of snow. Although, unlike snow, it won't disappear! It covers everything and can make breathing very difficult.

What's that smell?

Another danger can be the build-up of sulphur gas, which you'll recognise by its smell of rotten eggs. In which case, gas masks are essential, but even if you avoid sulphur gas, beware of carbon dioxide! This odourless gas builds up in hollows and can be deadly.

Is it raining?

Some volcanoes spit out clusters of lava called lapilli, which means 'little stones'. They are between 2 and 64 mm in size, and, depending on the strength of the eruption, they can be hurled quite far. Dodging lapilli is very difficult, and of course they are also extremely hot!

Anyone smell burning?

And just when you consider yourself on safe ground, you may need to watch where you put your feet. The ground may look solid, but hot magma could be running underneath it!

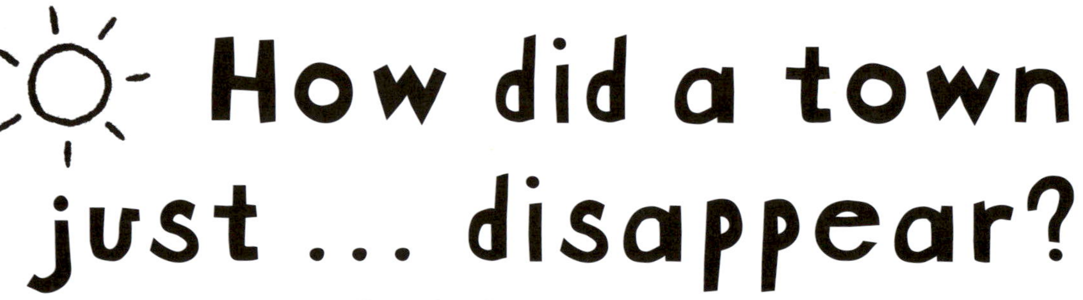

How did a town just ... disappear?

Pompeii, outside Naples in Italy, was a large, prosperous town. In CE 79 the town was almost completely destroyed when the nearby volcano, Vesuvius, erupted.

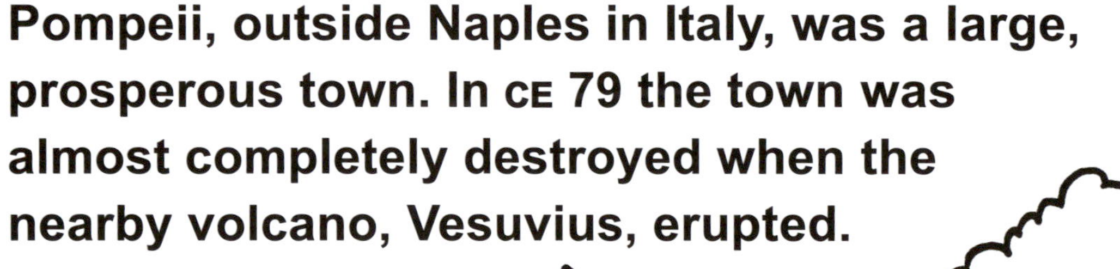

Pompeii was smothered in ash and lapilli, which rained down onto the town. This was followed by a great rolling cloud of hot ash and gases, roasting everything in its path. Even those who took shelter in their houses weren't safe.

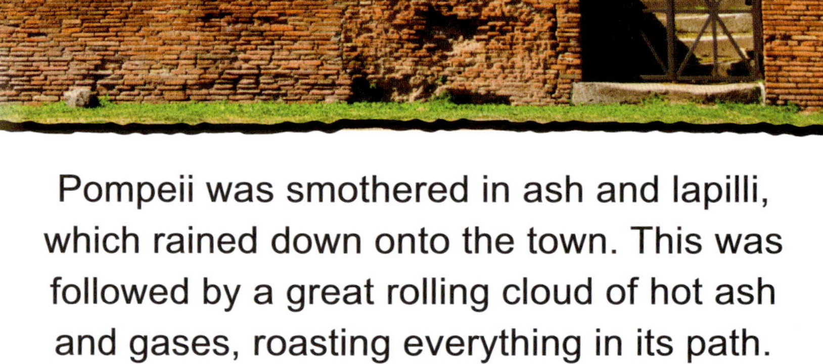

Pompeii was completely buried and eventually forgotten.

A deadly cloud

A hot volcanic cloud of ash and gases that travels at high speed is called a pyroclastic flow. It can reach up to 300 km/h and can be as hot as 500°C!

Look what I've found!

It wasn't until the 18th century that ancient coins and jewellery were found in the area. The King of Naples ordered an excavation. Gradually, Pompeii's buildings were revealed, and the secrets of life in the buried town were uncovered.

Well-cooked food

Nearly the whole town had been preserved in a thick layer of ash and pumice (a light form of hardened lava, full of holes.) This covering preserved many of the ancient wall paintings and floor mosaics, as well as everyday items used by the people who lived there.

Amazing things were discovered at Pompeii, including ancient bread, figs and eggs that were buried in the ash. You wouldn't want to eat them, though – the bread and figs are charcoal and the eggs are very well done!

Bread

Figs

Eggs

How violent is Mount Vesuvius?

That is a good question! Nearly three million people live in the city of Naples, which lies in the shadow of Mount Vesuvius. Scientists can't predict when Vesuvius will next erupt, which is why it is one of the most observed volcanoes in the world.

Be prepared

In case of an eruption, plans are in place to evacuate up to 700,000 people from Naples in under 72 hours. About 500 buses and over 200 trains will be used to take people away. If Vesuvius becomes active, they will inform residents of the risk using an **INTERNATIONAL RISK SCALE**.

International Risk Scale

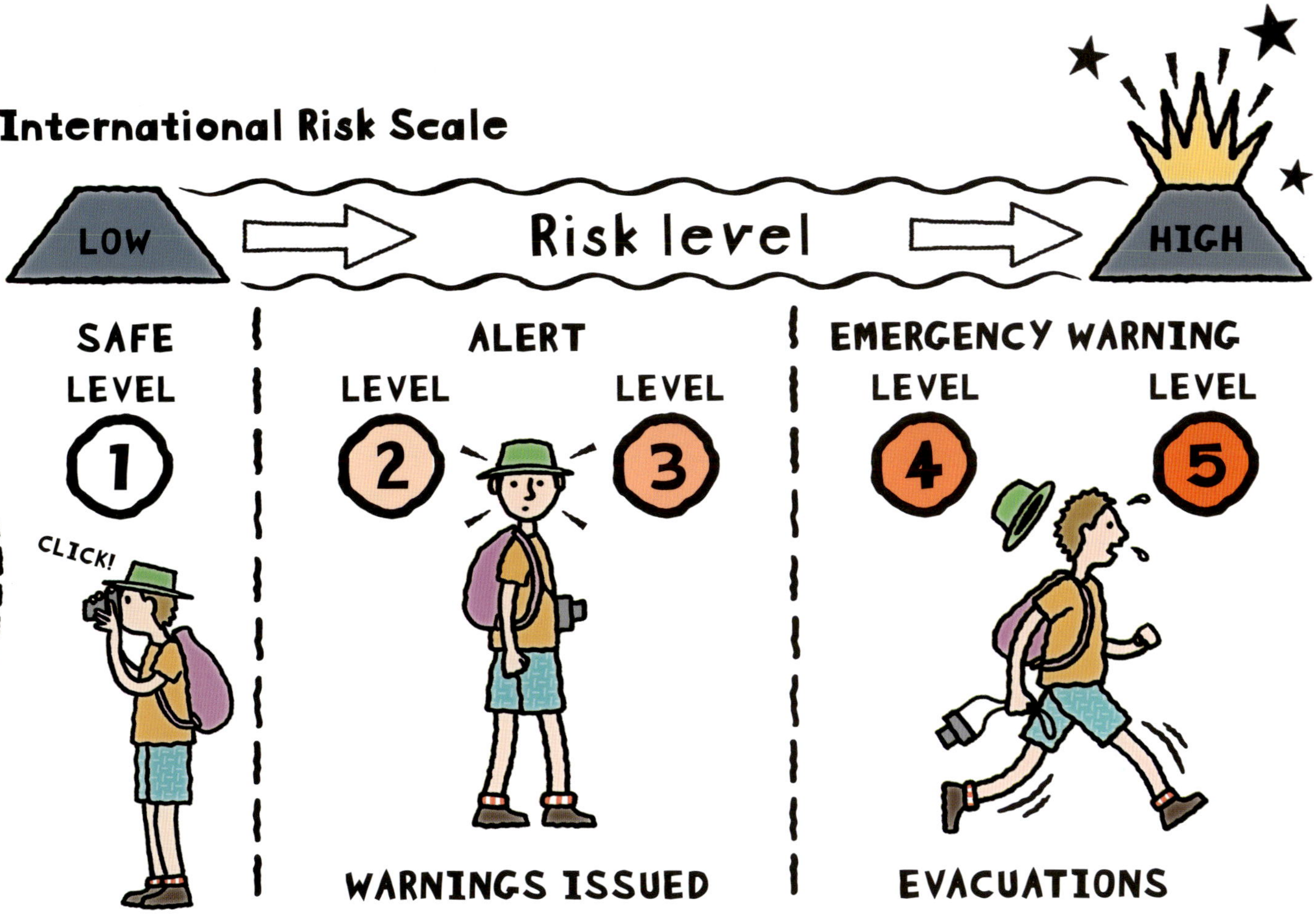

Evacuate!

People who live in an area that is affected by the movement of tectonic plates need to be prepared for an evacuation. They will often have a 'grab bag' of important items that can be taken in an emergency.

An emergency grab bag usually includes water and food, a first aid kit, cash and a phone charger.

Many countries have developed systems that send an early warning to mobile phones. The alert will inform people of the particular danger and what they should do.

What's in a volcanologist's bag?

Volcanologists are scientists who study volcanoes. They are constantly observing active volcanoes around the world to be able to predict eruptions. Volcanologists rely on all sorts of equipment in their work.

Moving ...

One of the earliest warnings of a future eruption is whether there has been any movement around the volcano. A **SEISMOGRAPH** records any tremors or 'rumblings' that may have occurred.

A seismograph reading showing a tremor.

Swelling ...

A **TILTMETER** can tell if the ground is swelling, as this is an indication that magma may be building up underground.

Essential tool

It's important to regularly collect rock and lava samples, as the content of the lava will change and it can indicate how severe future eruptions might be. So a trusty hammer should always be at hand.

Suited for the job

Sometimes volcanologists have to approach the volcano in order to collect samples. For this, they may need to wear a special heatproof suit. These suits are designed to resist temperatures of up to 1,500°C. There are boots and gloves to match. Using the suit, volcanologists can collect the latest lava samples.

Dante II the rescue!

Some of the dangerous work of predicting eruptions can be undertaken by a robot called Dante II. This includes temperature checks to see whether there is any change in a volcano's heat.

Dante II can also detect if there is build-up of gas – a strong indicator that an eruption is due!

Are volcanoes tourist magnets?

Surprisingly, yes they are! Volcanoes bring in tourists, which creates jobs. Tourists require tour guides, food, accommodation – and they will of course want to shop for souvenirs!

Wind-up Mt Fuji

The star of selfies

In Japan, Mount Fuji is believed to be sacred. Up to 300,000 people climb this active volcano every year! The last major eruption was over 300 years ago and Mount Fuji is one of Japan's most important tourist destinations. Don't worry, though – you don't have to climb it, you can just take a selfie in front of it!

Take a bath

Bathing in hot springs attracts tourists from around the world. Magma heats water deep underground, which finds its way through cracks to the Earth's surface. The ancient Romans used natural hot springs to fill their swimming-pool-sized public baths.

One hundred years or so after arriving in Britain, the Romans had built baths in a place we now call Bath!

Having a blast

Another big tourist attraction are geysers, where hot water, heated by volcanic rocks, builds up underground and then bursts high into the air. Old Faithful, in Yellowstone National Park, USA, got its name because its eruptions are very regular – up to 20 times a day!

Beware giants!

In Northern Ireland, 40,000 hexagonal rock columns attract hundreds of thousands of visitors every year. The legend is that the columns were created by Finn McCool, an Irish giant, and that's how they got their name – the Giant's Causeway. But the strangely shaped basalt rocks were actually created by volcanic action about 50 to 60 million years ago!

How do volcanoes grow tasty tomatoes?

It would be a shame not to make use of all the heat, energy and nutrients that volcanoes produce. In many places people do – in fact, crops have been grown on Mount Vesuvius since Roman times!

Vesuvio Piennolo cherry tomatoes

Topping tomatoes

Locals who grow their veg on the slopes of Mount Vesuvius reckon that their Vesuvio Piennolo cherry tomatoes are unique because of their sweetness. Scientists say this can be explained because the soil here contains minerals such as potassium and magnesium, stemming from volcanic ash and lava. Which makes these tomatoes absolutely perfect on a pizza!

A bananas idea

How about growing bananas in Iceland? Bananas prefer a warm, tropical climate and that certainly is not the case in Iceland (the clue is in the name!)!

Bananas

However, bananas **ARE** grown in Iceland alongside tomatoes, cucumbers and strawberries – all of which require an ice-free climate.

So how is this possible?

This is where volcanoes come in.

All these warmth-loving plants are grown in heated greenhouses. Iceland is one of the most volcanically active places on Earth. Activity deep underground is used to heat water that is then pumped around the greenhouses. It emerges as steam or hot water which can be collected. This is called **GEOTHERMAL ENERGY**.

Geo (Greek) = Earth
Thermos (Greek) = hot

Bananas growing in heated greenhouses in the Icelandic winter.

Heated outdoor swimming pools in Reykjavik, Iceland.

Heated cities

But it's not only useful for greenhouses – geothermal energy is used to heat 90 per cent of all houses in Iceland. Winter also can't stop outdoor sports, as pitches are heated by geothermal energy.

Volcanic electricity

It doesn't stop there, because the steam from geothermal energy is also used to drive turbines that produce electricity. This means that lighting and other services that use electricity are powered by clean, sustainable energy. **Well done Iceland!**

How do monkeys handle hot springs?

Thermal hot springs are not just enjoyed by humans! The monkeys in Ligokudani Park in northern Japan saw people bathing in hot spring baths and decided to do the same. The park was created to protect the monkeys living there, and now they have their own outdoor pools!

Why do some people love a muddy bath?

People have been taking volcanic mud baths for centuries. Volcanic mud is rich in minerals like sulphur, magnesium and zinc, and is used in some forms of skin therapy. Mud facials and body treatments can be found in spas around the world. You can even buy volcanic mud in jars to take home!

Can you surf on a volcano?

Yes, some dare-devils surf down the slopes of volcanoes! Surfers use a special board and are advised to avoid falling off, as the ash can contain small pieces of glass (ouch). The volcanoes also release gases, and occasionally lava bombs, because they are usually active, so volcano surfing is not likely to become an Olympic sport anytime soon!

Can animals predict volcanic eruptions?

Maybe. There are plenty of reports of animals fleeing an area just before an eruption. Goat herders near Mt Etna in Sicily reported that their animals got nervous many hours before a volcanic eruption and fled to safety. Small tremors often take place before an eruption and animals are very sensitive to any kind of vibration, so this could help explain it.

Glossary

Composite volcano A steep, cone-shaped volcano built up of many layers of rocks, ash and lava.

Dormant Describing a volcano that has not erupted for thousands of years, but could do so in the future.

Earthquake Violent shaking of the ground caused by movements in the Earth's crust.

Earth's crust The thin outer layer of rock surrounding our planet.

Effusive A volcanic eruption where lava flows easily down the sides of the volcano.

Eruption The pouring out of lava, rock and ash from a volcano.

Explosive A violent eruption where the lava is often under high pressure.

Extinct Describing a volcano not expected to ever erupt again.

Geothermal energy Heat energy from deep below the Earth's surface.

Geyser Hot spring that sends jets of water and steam into the air.

Lapilli Very small pieces of lava between 2 and 60 mm in size, thrown out of a volcano.

Lava Magma after it reaches the surface of a volcano.

Magma Molten rock beneath Earth's surface.

Mantle The hot layer under the Earth's crust where magma comes from.

Plug Created when magma cools and blocks the vent of the volcano.

Pyroclastic flow Very hot mixture of rocks, ash and steam moving at speed down the side of a volcano.

Seismograph Instrument that measures and records the intensity of earthquakes.

Shield volcano Volcano that has gentle sloping sides created when the lava flows a long way before cooling.

Sustainable energy Energy that is generated without using up natural resources such as coal, gas or oil.

Tectonic plate Giant piece of Earth's crust that floats on the mantle and pushes against the other plates.

Tiltmeter Instrument that measures the degree to which the ground swells in the build-up to a volcanic eruption.

Vent A place where lava emerges from a volcano.

Volcano An opening on the Earth's surface through which ash, rocks and lava can be ejected during an eruption.

Volcanologist A scientist who studies volcanoes.

Further reading

Websites

**natgeokids.com/uk/discover/geography/
physical-geography/volcano-facts**
Learn more explosive facts about volcanoes.

primaryhomeworkhelp.co.uk/mountains/volcanoes.htm
Lots of interesting facts and figures about volcanoes around the world.

kids.britannica.com/kids/article/volcano/353902
Interesting information and plenty of useful diagrams and pictures,
as well as video clips of erupting volcanoes.

dkfindout.com/uk/earth/structure-earth
Amazing pictures and diagrams of a volcano, the structure of the Earth and much more.

Books

DKfindout! Volcanoes
(DK books 2016)

Pop-Up Volcano!
by Fleur Daugey (Thames and Hudson, 2020)

The Explosive History of Volcanoes
by Clive Gifford (Franklin Watts, 2023)

Geographics: Volcanoes
by Izzi Howell (Franklin Watts, 2018)

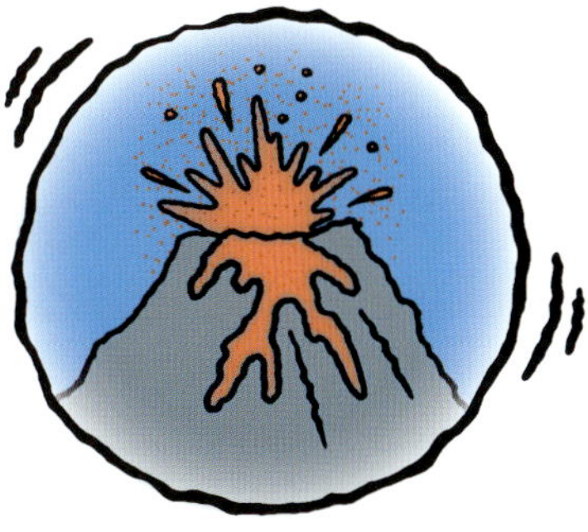

Index